W9-BFK-246

ZÜLAL AYTÜRE-SCHEELE

P·A·P·E·R·F·O·L·D·I·N·G   F·U·N

ORIGAMI
IN COLOR

GALLERY BOOKS
An Imprint of W. H. Smith Publishers Inc.
112 Madison Avenue
New York City 10016

C ▾ O ▴ N ▾ T ▴ E ▾ N ▴ T ▾ S

First published by Octopus Books Ltd.

This edition published in 1986 by Gallery Books
An imprint of W. H. Smith Publishers Inc.
112 Madison Avenue, New York, New York 10016

© 1986 Falken-Verlag GmbH Niedernhausen/Ts.
    West Germany
© 1986 English translation Ridgmount Books Ltd.

Translated by Linda Sonntag

Produced by Mandarin Publishers Ltd.
22a Westlands Road
Quarry Bay, Hong Kong

Reprinted 1987

ISBN 0 8317 6670 0

Printed in Hong Kong

FOREWORD

Origami is the Japanese art of paper-folding. It was first practised almost a thousand years ago at the Imperial Court, where it was considered an amusing and elegant way of passing the time. Over the centuries the skill was passed down to the ordinary people, who took it up with enthusiasm and made it into a folk art. Today in Japan the art of paper-folding is as widely practised by children, parents and grandparents as it was centuries ago. And for a number of years now origami has been immensely popular here in the West too. This book will enable you to join the many thousands of people who have already discovered the enjoyment this inexpensive hobby provides.

Eyecatching models – animals, masks, flowers and decorations – are made by simply folding coloured paper. Origami demands concentration, stimulates the imagination and develops dexterity of the fingertips. Apart from that, it's great fun to see a square of paper transformed with a few folds into a pretty flower or a lifelike animal.

Origami can also be put to practical use. You can use the models to make an attractive mobile for a child's bedroom, or you can present someone with a magnificent bunch of flowers on their birthday. You can make masks for carnivals or parties. In this book there are 36 different models to make, based on seven basic shapes.

Here's wishing you a lot of fun in discovering origami.

Zülal Aytüra-Scheele

ORIGAMI PAPER

Japanese shops offer a huge selection of different coloured origami papers. They can be patterned or plain – or plain on one side and patterned on the other. There are large sheets that can be cut down to the size you require, and smaller sheets designed to be worked with straight away. The paper comes in various strengths and qualities. To get genuine Japanese origami paper you don't have to go as far as Japan. It is now available in many stationery shops in this country.

But you can make the models out of lots of different kinds of paper, including good quality gift wrap. When buying paper for origami, you need to make sure that it will fold well and hold a good crease.

It shouldn't tear, stretch or bend when you fold it, so it needs to be both firm and thin.

Buying your paper, choosing patterns and colours to suit the models you are going to make, is a pleasure in itself. Once you have a little experience in paper-folding, you will find that selecting the paper is as much a part of the art of origami as folding it.

Use whatever paper you like to make the models in this book. Special papers are specified where they are required.

GOLDEN RULES

To start off with, here are a few rules to follow to make paper-folding easier.

1 Always work on a smooth flat surface.
2 Measure your paper exactly and cut it accurately and cleanly.
3 Make your folds carefully. Run your thumbnail along the crease each time you make a fold to make it sharp.
4 Begin by folding the basic shape required for the model you have chosen. You will find it more convenient to work through the book from beginning to end, as some models are based partially on previous ones.
5 The instruction steps should be followed in sequence. They won't make sense if read in isolation.
6 If one of your folds – or even a whole model – goes wrong, don't lose heart. Go through all the steps carefully one by one, checking that you have followed the instructions properly and not missed a vital word or overlooked an arrow or dotted line.

FOLDING PRACTICE

Folding paper is not difficult, but it does get easier with practice. Get your fingers on the right track with the exercise below. Remember, the neater your folds, the better all your models will look.

Please don't lose heart if you are not successful straight away with this exercise. It is essential to persevere until you master the knack; this should take no more than 10–15 minutes. Once you have got the hang of these key paper-folding techniques you will be ready to tackle with confidence the wide variety of paper models featured on the pages that follow.

1 Start with a square of paper.

2 Fold it in half diagonally towards you. Now fold the lefthand edges in to meet the diagonal crease.

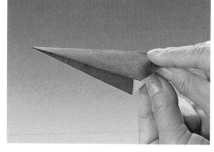

3 Fold the top and bottom halves together, with the white side of the paper inside.

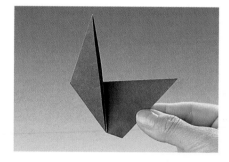

4 Fold the lefthand side up so that the point is vertical. Make a crease and ...

5 ... fold it back again. Open up the shape from beneath and ...

6 ... fold the lefthand point ...

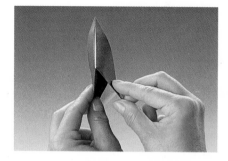

7 ... outwards, to where you made the crease in step 3.

By practising these folds you have already made a simple duck.

8 Firm along the fold. Fold the top point ...

9 ... over to the left.

10 Unfold the point again and open it out a little.

11 Fold the point along the crease you have just made ...

12 ... over and down ...

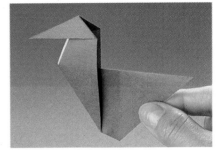

13 ... to the left.

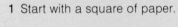

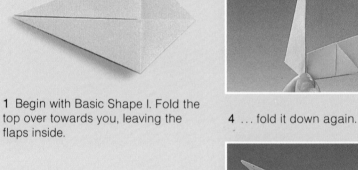

BASIC SHAPE I

SWAN

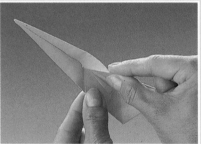

4 … fold it down again.

1 Start with a square of paper.

1 Begin with Basic Shape I. Fold the top over towards you, leaving the flaps inside.

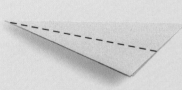

2 Fold it towards you diagonally in the middle.

2 Fold the paper up along the dotted line. Repeat on the other side.

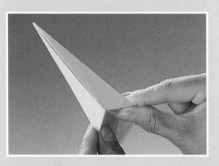

5 Open the shape out from beneath.

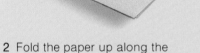

3 Fold the lefthand edges in to meet the diagonal crease. This is Basic Shape I.

3 Fold the lefthand point up along the dotted line. Make a crease and …

6 Along the crease you've just made, fold the left side of the shape …

7 … upwards. Along the line indicated, fold the point …

11 On the two lines indicated …

15 … fold the tail forwards …

8 … down to the left. Make a crease.

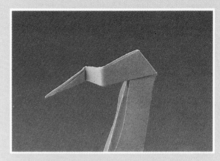

12 … make parallel folds.

16 … and inwards along the crease.

9 Unfold it again, opening out the point.

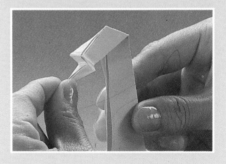

13 Fold the paper inwards on the first crease, and outwards on the second.

17 Pull the point of the tail up, press it in towards the centre and make a fold to hold it there.

10 Fold the point over to the left along the crease you have just made.

14 On the line indicated …

18 The finished swan.

CYGNET

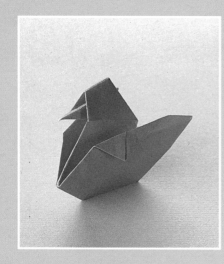

1 Start with Basic Shape I (p.8). Fold the white triangle along the dotted line ...

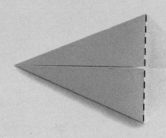

2 ... in to the left. Fold the left point along the dotted line ...

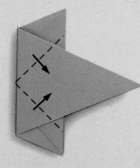

3 ... in to the right. Fold the lefthand top and bottom sections in along the dotted lines ...

4 ... to meet at the horizontal centre fold.

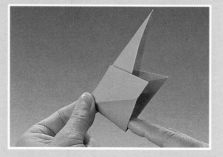

5 Pick up the shape and open it out from underneath.

6 Fold the two wings together.

7 Fold the wingtip down on the dotted line. Repeat on the other side. Fold the front bottom point up on the lower dotted line.

8 Make a crease on the dotted line.

9 Open the point out and fold it over to the left along the crease.

10 Open the shape out along the bottom fold and press the small triangle inwards. Fold the head in on the first line ...

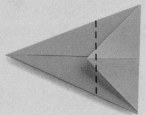

11 ... and out on the second line. The cygnet is finished.

4 … to the right.
Working on the righthand triangle …

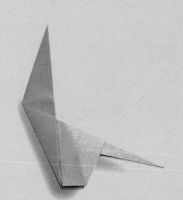

9 Open up the lefthand side of the shape …

5 … fold the bottom section up along the dotted line …

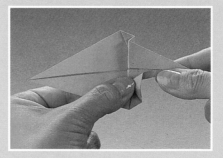

6 … and fold flat the small triangle that has formed at the left.

10 … and bring the top down, folding it flat.

BABY MONKEY

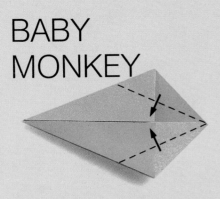

1 Start with Basic Shape I (p.8). Fold the righthand top and bottom sections in on the dotted lines …

2 … to meet at the horizontal centre fold. At the arrows, fold the righthand point …

7 Repeat on the righthand side. Fold the top down …

11 Make three parallel folds along the lines indicated. Fold the first in, the second out, and the third in.

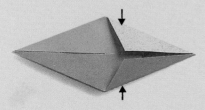

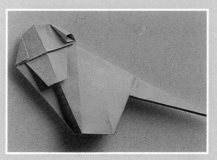

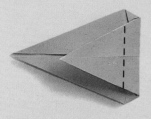

3 … in to the left. Fold it back along the dotted line …

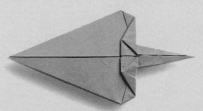

8 … to meet the bottom. Fold the lefthand point up on the dotted line.

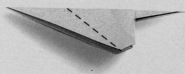

12 Fold the top right and lefthand corners forward and round them out to form ears. The baby monkey is ready.

4 ... over to the left. Fold the top half over along the centre fold to meet the bottom half.

5 Fold the lefthand point along the dotted line ...

6 ... over and up.

PEACOCK

THE PAPER

A A small sheet of paper for the body (about 10 × 10 cm)

B A second sheet of paper, four times bigger than the first, for the tail (about 20 × 20 cm)

C A very small piece of paper for the crown (about 3 × 3 cm)

THE BODY

1 Make Basic Shape I (p.8) with paper A. Along the dotted lines fold the righthand top ...

2 ... and bottom sections in to meet at the horizontal centre fold. Turn the shape over.

3 Fold the righthand point along the dotted line ...

7 Open out point from beneath ...

8 ... and fold it up and out along the crease you have already made.

12

9 Fold the point over on the line indicated.

10 Open up the point.

11 Fold the point over to the left on the crease you have just made.

12 Now the body is ready.

THE TAIL

1 Take paper B and fold it in accordion pleats.

2 Fold it in half.

3 Slot the body in place between the two halves of the tail. Stick the centre edges of the tail together with glue.

THE CROWN

1 Take paper C and fold it in accordion pleats.

2 Fold it in half and stick the centre edges together with glue.

3 Stick the crown in place on the peacock's head.

PENGUIN

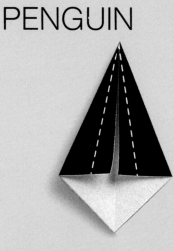

1 Start with Basic Shape I (p.8). Along the dotted lines ...

2 ... fold the right and left wings outwards. Turn the shape over.

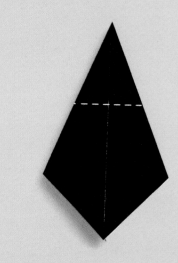

3 Fold the top point down along the dotted line.

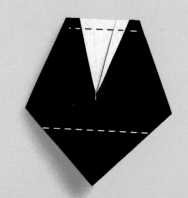

4 Fold the top and bottom points up along the dotted lines.

5 Fold the shape in half along the centre fold.

6 Take the top point ...

7 ... and pull it down to the right. Make a fold to hold it there.

14

8 Fold the point along the line indicated ...

11 Fold the point out along the crease you have just made.

14 Fold the wing along the dotted line to the left. Repeat on the other side.

9 ... over to the left.

12 Make two parallel folds along the lines indicated.

15 Fold the front righthand section of the figure inwards along the dotted line. Repeat on the other side.

10 Open out the fold.

13 Fold the point to the left along the first line, and to the right along the second.

16 The penguin is now finished.

JUNGLE SCENE

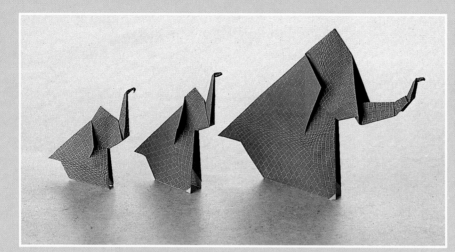

ELEPHANT

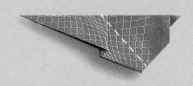

7 Make a crease along the dotted line.

8 Open out the shape from beneath.

9 Fold the paper out along the crease you have already made.

1 Begin with Basic Shape I (p.8). Fold the righthand corner along the dotted line ...

4 Fold the lefthand point along the dotted line to the right.

2 ... to the left. Fold the point along the dotted line ...

5 Fold the point back along the dotted line ...

3 ... back to the right. Turn the shape over.

6 ... to the left. Fold the shape in half along the centre fold.

10 Make a crease along the dotted line.

11 Open out the head a little from beneath.

15 ... in. Repeat on the other side.

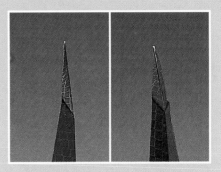

19 Fold the end of the trunk to the left along the line indicated. Open the point out above the fold ...

12 Fold the point inwards on the crease you have already made.

16 Along the dotted line, pull the trunk ...

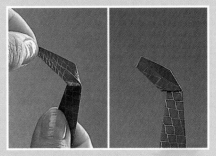

20 ... and turn it to the left, making a rhomboid shape. Make a fold to hold it there and fold the tip inwards once again.

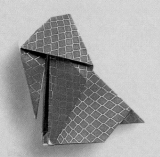

13 Make sharp creases on the lines indicated.

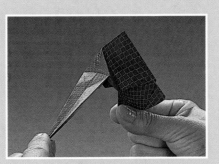

17 ... out and up.

14 Open the paper out and push the resulting small triangle ...

18 Press the trunk flat and make a fold to hold it there.

21 Fold both ears forwards, and the elephant is finished.

PIRATE MASK

1 Begin with Basic Shape I (p.8). Along the dotted line, fold the inner righthand corner ...

PUPPY

1 Begin with step 10 of the elephant (p.18). Make two parallel folds along the lines indicated.

2 Fold the lefthand point in at the righthand line, and out at the lefthand line.

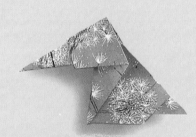

3 Fold the lefthand point in at the line indicated.

4 The finished puppy.

2 ... down. Fold the upper and lower points towards the centre on the dotted lines.

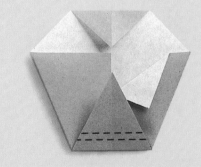

3 Make two folds along the dotted lines. Pull the triangle out, fold it back inwards on the lower line, and out again on the upper line.

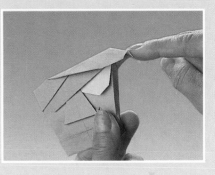

8 Fold the headscarf along dotted line 2 …

9 … to give it a knotted effect.

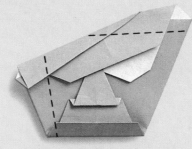

4 Lay the triangle back against the shape. Fold the top down along the dotted line. Fold the tip of the eyepatch back with the arrow. For the nose, make two parallel folds.

6 Fold the headscarf forwards over the eyepatch. Fold the lefthand side of the figure back along the dotted line.

10 Pull out the nose.

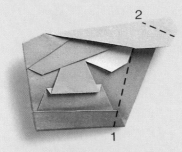

5 Fold the tip of the triangle down and inwards along the upper dotted line, and fold it up and out again along the lower dotted line. Fold the headscarf forwards along the dotted line.

7 Fold the righthand side of the figure back along dotted line 1.

11 Paint the eyepatch black and the headscarf red, and the pirate mask is complete.

DECORATIONS

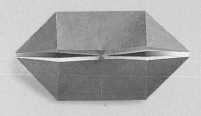

BASIC SHAPE II

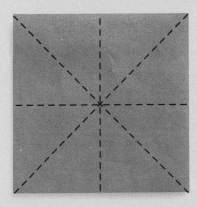

1 Fold a square piece of paper into eight along the dotted lines indicated. Open it out again.

2 Fold the right and left sides in together along the vertical centre fold, white side inside.

3 Fold the upper and lower sections in together along the horizontal centre fold. Unfold them.

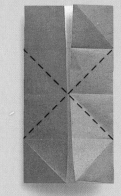

4 Along the dotted lines, fold the shape first to the right ...

5 ... and then to the left.

6 Lift the inner lower corners up and out.

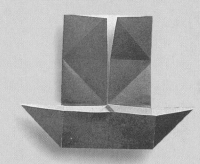

7 Fold up the lower edge of the shape to meet the horizontal centre fold.

8 Turn the shape upside down and repeat steps 6 and 7.

9 This is Basic Shape II.

WINDMILL

POMANDER

1 Begin with Basic Shape II (p.23). Along the dotted lines . . .

3 The finished windmill.

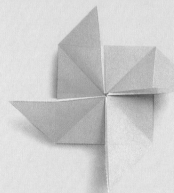

1 Begin with a windmill.

2 . . . fold the lefthand triangle up and the righthand triangle down.

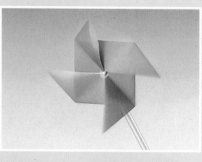

4 You can fix the windmill to a stick with a pin or small nail. Blow, and it will turn.

2 Lift one of the sails vertically upwards.

24

3 Open it out …

7 … open it out …

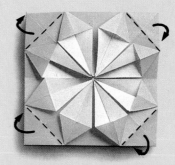

9 Fold the four corners of the shape back along the dotted lines.

4 … and press it together with the point inwards. Repeat with the other three sails.

8 … and press it down flat. Repeat with the lefthand fold. Repeat for each square.

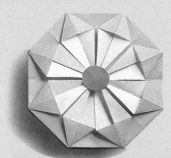

10 Stick a round piece of paper in the middle of the flower.

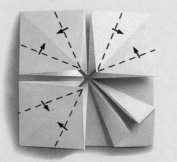

5 Fold the inner two edges of each small square over on the dotted lines to meet at the centre.

6 Lift the righthand fold vertically …

11 Make six flowers and stick them together at the corners to form a ball. The pomander is complete.

ANGEL FISH

You will need a square sheet of paper. If you don't want the mouth of the fish to be white, cut another equal sized square of paper in the colour of your choice and stick the two sheets together, white sides inwards.

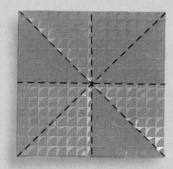

1 Fold the paper along the lines indicated. Unfold it again.

3 From here, work as for Basic Shape II (p.23). First fold the right and left sides in . . .

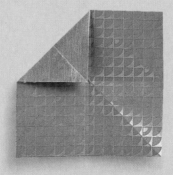

2 Fold the top lefthand corner down to the centre point. Turn the shape over.

4 . . . to meet at the vertical centre fold. Then fold the upper and lower sections in . . .

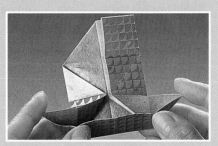

5 ... to meet at the horizontal centre fold.

9 Lift the inner bottom corners up and pull them out.

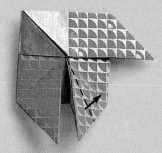

13 Fold the lower righthand point up along the dotted line.

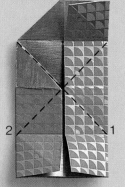

6 Fold them back out again. Fold the lower left side of the shape along dotted line 1 ...

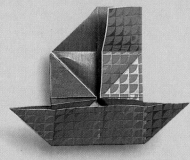

10 Fold up the lower edge of the shape to meet the horizontal centre fold.

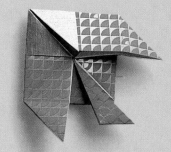

14 Turn the shape over ...

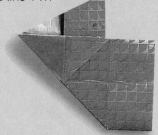

7 ... up and over to the right.

11 Pull the top point out and down so that the upper edge of the shape meets the horizontal centre fold.

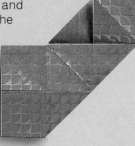

8 Unfold it. Fold the lower right side of the shape along dotted line 2, up and over to the left. Unfold it.

12 Fold the lower two triangles down on the dotted lines.

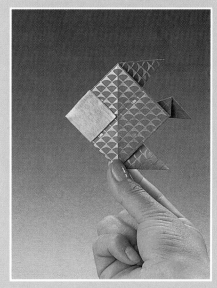

15 ... and the angel fish appears.

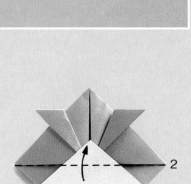

BASIC SHAPE III

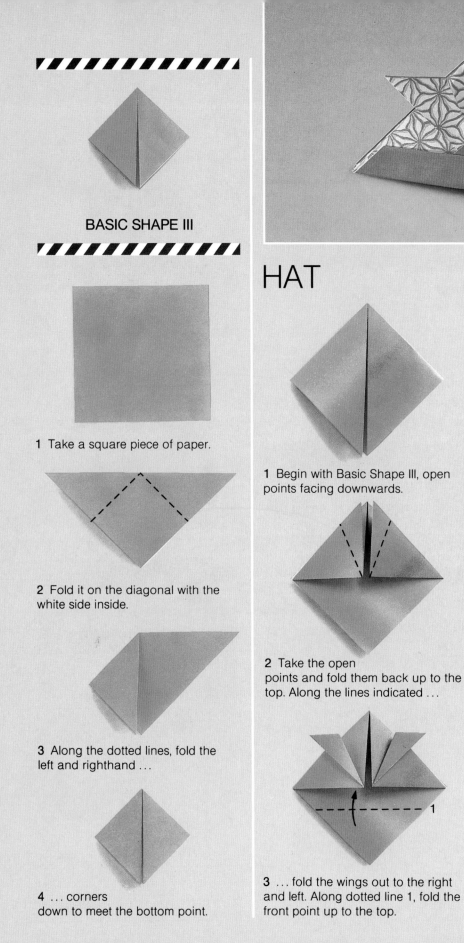

1 Take a square piece of paper.

2 Fold it on the diagonal with the white side inside.

3 Along the dotted lines, fold the left and righthand ...

4 ... corners down to meet the bottom point.

HAT

1 Begin with Basic Shape III, open points facing downwards.

2 Take the open points and fold them back up to the top. Along the lines indicated ...

3 ... fold the wings out to the right and left. Along dotted line 1, fold the front point up to the top.

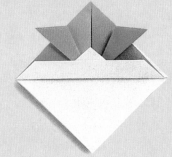

4 Along dotted line 2, fold the paper up again.

5 Fold the remaining lower triangle to the back.

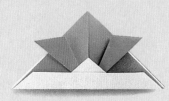

6 The finished hat.

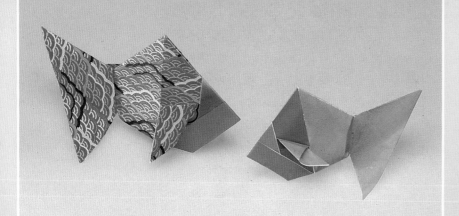

7 Open up the shape.

GOLDFISH

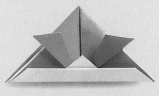

1 Start with the hat.

4 Measure three-quarters of the way along the lower righthand side ...

8 Pull the tail down from the top corner and fold it out.

2 Open it out ...

5 ... and cut along the fold to that point.

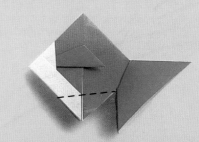

9 Fold the lower edge of this side of the fish in along the dotted line. Repeat with the other side.

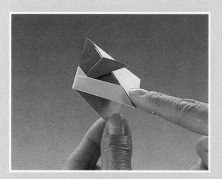

3 ... and fold both the sides together.

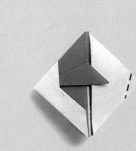

6 Make a sharp fold along the line indicated.

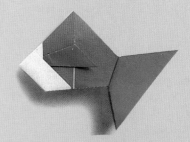

10 The finished goldfish.

Variation
You can fold the fin down and paint the mouth or cover it with coloured paper.

BASIC SHAPE IV

TUG

1 Take a square sheet of paper and fold it into four along the dotted lines. Unfold it. Fold each corner ...

1 Begin with Basic Shape IV. Turn the shape over.

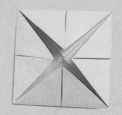

4 Fold the four outer corners ...

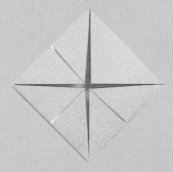

2 ... in to the centre.

2 Fold the four corners ...

5 ... in to the centre. Turn the shape over.

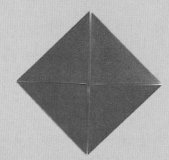

3 This is Basic Shape IV.

3 ... in to the centre. Turn the shape over again.

6 Now you have four small squares within one larger one.

30

7 Open out one of the small squares.

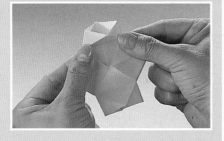

8 Repeat with the square opposite. These are the two funnels.

9 Pull the central corners of the remaining two squares to the outside, bringing the two funnels together.

10 Colour in the rings around the funnels. The tug is now ready to float.

SANTA

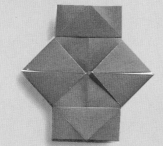

1 Begin with step 8 of the tug (the two funnels are above and below).

2 Open out a third square ...

3 ... and press it flat.

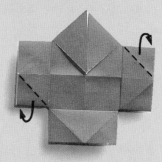

4 Fold the paper in along the dotted lines ...

5 ... to make the arms.

6 The fourth square forms the head. Paint Santa's face, add a beard and trim the coat. He's ready.

TABLE DECORATIONS

PICTURE FRAME

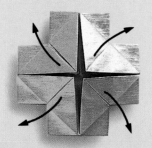

1 Begin with step 8 of the tug (p.31). Open up the two remaining closed squares …

2 … and press them flat. Turn the shape over.

3 Fold outwards the four corners that meet at the centre.

4 Turn the shape over.

5 There is a rectangle on each side of the square. Lift one outer corner of one of the rectangles …

6 … vertically upwards …

7 … open it out, and press it down flat.

8 Repeat with the other outer corner of this rectangle. Repeat with the other three rectangles. The picture frame is ready.
As a variation, turn back the four corners on the dotted lines.

9 You can hang the frame up or, if you turn it round and half open two of the large triangles at the back, it will stand up on its own.

BASIC SHAPE V

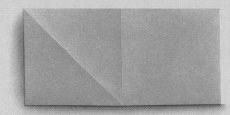

3 Fold the paper in half, white side inwards.

7 Fold it out flat. Lift the left wing across . . .

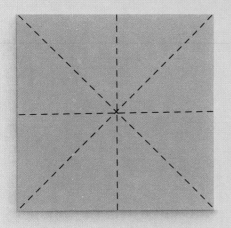

1 Fold a square piece of paper twice across the centre and twice diagonally . . .

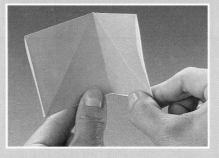

4 Lift the right half of the paper at 90° to the left half . . .

8 . . . to join the right one.

5 . . . open it out . . .

9 Repeat steps 3–6 with the left half of the shape.

2 . . . then unfold it again.

6 . . . and press it apart.

10 This is Basic Shape V.

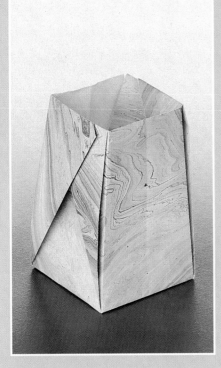

VASE

3 Fold the protruding triangle over along the dotted line ...

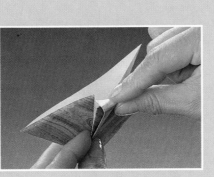

4 ... inside the shape.

7 Make a sharp crease along the dotted line.

8 Open out the vase. Push the base into a square, using the crease you have just made.

1 Begin with Basic Shape V, point downwards. Along the dotted line, fold the upper left triangle over ...

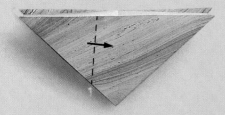

2 ... to the right. Fold the tip of this triangle over to the left along the dotted line.

5 Fold the upper righthand triangle to the left on dotted line 1. Fold its tip back to the right on dotted line 2.

6 Repeat steps 3 and 4. Turn the shape round and repeat the whole process on the reverse side.

9 The finished vase.

BUTTERFLY

Stick two equal sized squares of different coloured paper together and use as one sheet.

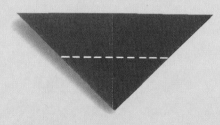

1 Start with Basic Shape V (p.34), point downwards.

2 Fold the point up along the dotted line and turn the shape over.

3 Open the shape out to reveal the inside.

4 Press the inside square shape flat. Fold the upper layers of the bottom half of the butterfly up along the dotted lines. Crease and fold back.

5 Open out the central square by lifting its bottom two corners over the creases towards the horizontal centre folds.

6 Press the new shape flat. Cut along the dotted line ...

7 ... to the centre. Fold the resulting triangles along the dotted lines ...

8 ... to the right and left.

9 Fold the shape in half.

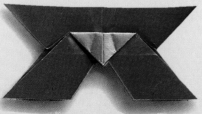

10 Open out the wings and fold them over, making a sharp crease along the dotted line. This is the simple butterfly.

11 For the more elaborate butterfly, open up the shape again and turn it over. Along the dotted line ...

12 ... fold the point down. Turn the shape over.

13 Along the dotted lines ...

14 ... fold the two wingtips down.

15 Fold the shape in half.

16 Open it out again. Using the fold lines, plump out the body and open up the wings to put the finishing touches to the butterfly.

5 Fold the front point along the dotted line to the centre.

6 Fold the two triangles along the dotted lines, making sharp creases.

BALLOON

7 Fit the top triangles into the side triangles. Repeat on the reverse side.

1 Begin with Basic Shape V (p.34), point upwards. Fold the front right and lefthand corners up along the dotted lines ...

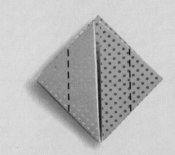

3 Turn the shape over and repeat on the reverse side. Make a crease along the horizontal. Fold the front right and lefthand triangles in along the dotted lines ...

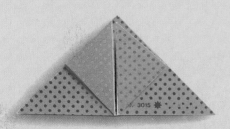

2 ... to meet at the top.

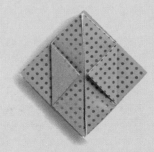

4 ... to the centre. Repeat on the reverse side.

8 Blow hard into the hole in the lower point to inflate the balloon.

3 Lift the righthand side of the paper 90° to the lefthand side . . .

6 Make a sharp crease. Fold the left wing over . . .

BASIC SHAPE VI

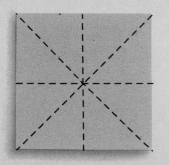

1 Fold a square of paper four times across the centre along the dotted lines, making sharp creases. Open it out.

4 . . . open it out and . . .

7 . . . to join the right wing.

8 Repeat steps 3–7 with the left half of the shape.

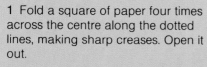

2 Fold it over diagonally, white side inside.

5 . . . press it down flat.

9 This is Basic Shape VI.

VIOLETS

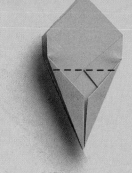

5 Repeat on the reverse side. Make a sharp crease along the dotted line.

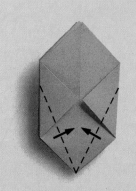

1 Start with Basic Shape VI, open point upwards. Fold the front left and righthand corners in along the dotted lines …

3 Fold the front lower triangles up along the dotted lines …

6 Open out the front of the shape.

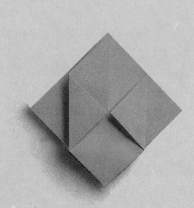

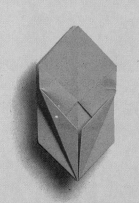

2 … to the middle. Repeat on the reverse side.

4 … so that the lower edges meet at the centre fold.

7 The violet is finished. Make a stem with a length of fine wire, push it up through the centre of the flower and loop it over to fix the stamens in place.

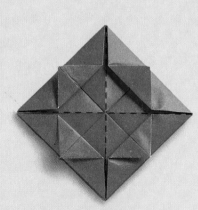

5 ... fold the four inner corners outwards so that they touch the centre of the four sides of the square. Now continue as for Basic Shape VI. Make two sharp creases along the dotted lines.

ROSE

The rose is made by combining the steps of Basic Shapes IV and VI.

1 Take a large square of paper (about 24 cm square) and fold it as shown. Unfold it.

3 Fold the four corners of the new square in to the centre point.

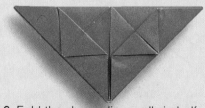

6 Fold the shape diagonally in half with the previous folds outermost.

2 Fold the four corners to the centre point, white side facing in.

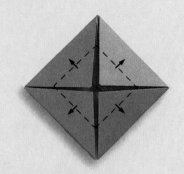

4 For the third time, fold the four corners to the centre point. Along the dotted lines ...

7 Lift the righthand side of the paper at 90° to the lefthand side ...

8 ... open it out ...

9 ... press it apart and fold it down.

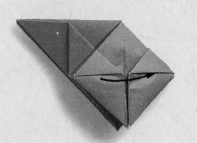

10 Fold the resulting lefthand wing across ...

11 ... to join the righthand wing. Turn the shape over. Repeat the folds from step 7.

12 New version of Basic Shape VI.

13 Hold the base of the shape open in your fingers.

14 Open out the four points.

15 Gently open out the outer petals.

16 Open the middle petals.

17 Do the same with the inner petals.

18 The rose is finished. Fix a wire stem to the base and wrap it round with green tape.

STAR-SHAPED BOX

5 … and press it down flat.

1 Start with Basic Shape VI (p.40), open point uppermost. Fold the front left and right triangles along the dotted lines …

3 Lift one of the wings diagonally …

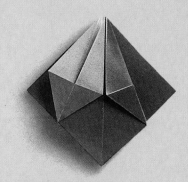

6 Crease it into place.

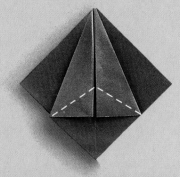

2 … in to the centre fold. Make two sharp creases along the dotted lines.

4 … open it out …

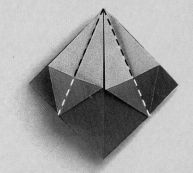

7 Repeat with the other wing. Turn the shape over and repeat steps 2–6 on the reverse side. Along the dotted lines …

8 ... fold both outer wings in to the centre.

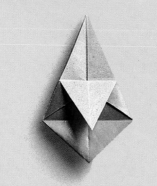

11 Fold the top front point down. Fold the top back point down behind the shape. Make sharp creases to hold the folds.

14 Using the foldlines, push out the square base of the box.

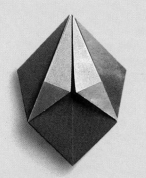

9 Press the shape flat, turn it over and repeat on the reverse side.

12 Pull the left and righthand points carefully apart, slowly opening the star-shaped box.

15 Firm up the base edges.

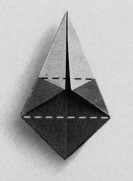

10 Make two sharp creases along the dotted lines.

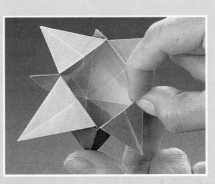

13 Firm up the top edges of the box.

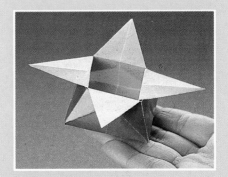

16 The finished box.

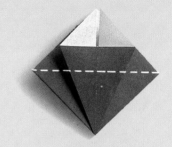

5 Press the folds in place. Make a sharp crease along the dotted line.

6 Fold the upper right and lefthand edges of the 'mouth' in to the vertical centre fold and open them again.

LILY

1 Begin with Basic Shape VI (p.40), open corner upwards. Make two sharp creases on the dotted lines.

3 ... open it out ...

7 Open the 'mouth'.

2 Lift the front righthand wing up vertically ...

4 ... and press it apart so that the vertical folds lie on top of one another and the shape looks like a mouth.

8 Press the corners of the 'mouth' inwards to the centre fold, so that the edges of the paper meet on the fold.

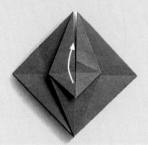

9 Press the shape flat. Fold the small triangle ...

13 Turn the shape over and repeat steps 2–12 on the reverse side. All four sides are now rhomboid in shape. On a plain unfolded side, along the dotted lines ...

17 Carefully pull out the left and righthand petals.

10 ... up on the horizontal centre line. Fold the left wing ...

14 ... fold the front lower left and righthand edges in to the centre.

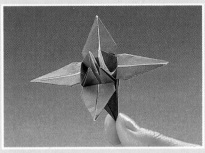

18 This is an iris.

11 ... across to meet the right.

15 Repeat step 14 on the other three unfolded sides. Make a sharp crease on the dotted line.

19 Curl the outer petals round a pencil, and the iris turns into ...

12 Repeat steps 2–11 with the front lefthand side.

16 Carefully pull apart the front and back petals.

20 ... a lily.

FROG

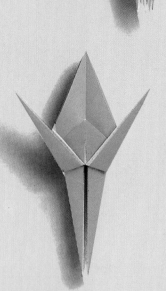

5 Repeat on the other three plain sides.

6 Starting on one of the sides shaped as shown, fold up the front two lower points on the dotted lines.

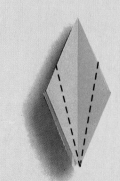

1 Follow instructions for the lily (p.46) up to step 9. Without folding the small triangle up, continue ...

3 ... so that you end with a rhombus. Starting on a plain unfolded side, fold the front left and righthand sections in on the dotted line ...

2 ... to step 13. Repeat this process with the other three sides ...

4 ... to the middle.

7 Unfold them again.

8 Open out the left and righthand wings.

9 Fold them up as shown and make a firm crease.

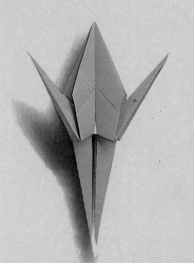

10 These are the frog's front legs.

11 Shape the forelegs and hindlegs by folding along the dotted lines. First for the hindlegs ...

12 ... fold along the dotted lines and make a crease. Unfold.

13 Open the outside of the leg.

14 Push it inside out through the same crease. Do the same with the knee bends. Fold up the foot. Fold up the forelegs twice as shown.

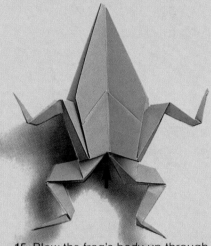

15 Blow the frog's body up through the hole between its back legs. Gently push into shape.

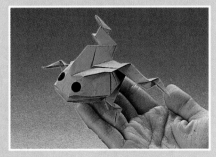

16 The finished frog. Paint or stick on its eyes.

5 ... until the central fold is at 90° to the spine of the upright triangle.

CRAB

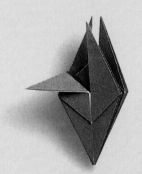

1 Begin with step 10 of the lily (p.47).

3 ... fold the front lefthand point out to the left. Unfold.

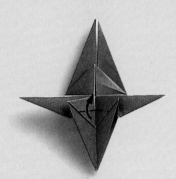

6 Fold the small triangle back into position. Repeat with the front right-hand point. Fold the tip of the small triangle up on the dotted line ...

2 Repeat these folds on the other three sides. Fold the small triangle down on the centre fold. On the dotted line ...

4 Open the wing from the outside and pull the point down ...

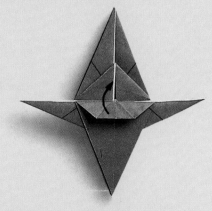

7 ... to the centre point. Make creases on the claws and back legs along the dotted lines.

8 Open up the right claw.

9 Turn the claw inside out along the crease line. Repeat with the other claws and the back legs.

10 Repeat steps 7–9 along the dotted lines.

11 Make sharp creases along the dotted lines.

12 Open out the two tiny top points. These are the eyes.

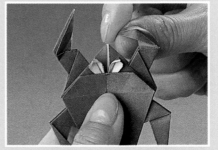

13 Turn the claw points over to the opposite side to round them out.

14 Turn the crab over.

15 Fold the top of the body to the inside on the dotted line. Fold the lower part of the body up on the upper line, and down on the lower line.

16 Turn the crab over again.

17 This is the finished crab.

WATERLILY

1 Take a sheet of thin paper about 24 cm square. Prefold the paper on the dotted lines.

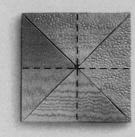

3 ... to meet at the middle. Make creases on the dotted lines.

4 Fold the shape diagonally in half.

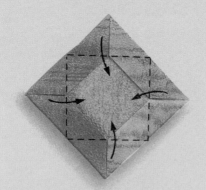

2 Fold the corners over on the first crease line to meet the second crease line. Fold the sides in again on the second crease line. Fold the four corners in ...

5 Lift the right half of the shape up vertically.

6 Open the fold and press it apart. Fold it flat.

7 Fold the resulting lefthand triangle over ...

8 ... to join the right.

9 Repeat steps 5–8 with the left half of the shape.

10 Lift the front righthand triangle vertically.

11 Open it out and fold it flat.

15 Push the left and righthand corners of the 'mouth' in to meet at the centre line.

19 Fold the front and back triangles out from the shape.

12 Make a crease along the centre line.

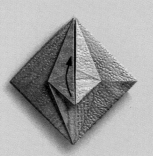

16 Fold the resulting small triangle up on the centre line . . .

20 Pull the right and lefthand points downwards.

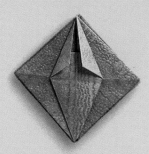

13 Fold the top right and lefthand sections of the inner 'mouth' shape over on the dotted lines to meet at the centre. Open them again.

17 . . . and the left wing over to meet the right.

21 Turn the shape upside down so that the open points are uppermost. Curl the petals round a pencil.

14 Open out the 'mouth' shape.

18 Repeat steps 9–17 with the other three sides.

22 Open the inner petals and curl them over.

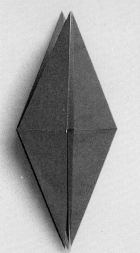

7 Flatten the left and righthand corners of the 'mouth' shape so that the sides meet in the middle.

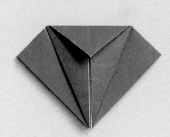

3 . . . fold the corner down.

BASIC SHAPE VII

4 Unfold the last three folds.

8 Make the creases sharp and turn the shape over. Repeat the folds on the reverse side.

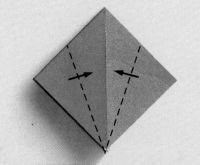

1 Begin with Basic Shape VI (p.40), open point downwards. Along the dotted lines . . .

5 Gently lift the lower front point.

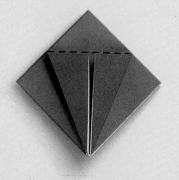

2 . . . fold the front left and righthand sections in to meet at the centre fold. Along the dotted line . . .

6 Fold the point up to the top on the crease you have already made.

9 This is Basic Shape VII.

FLYING CRANE

5 Fold the lefthand point inside out on the crease you have just made. This is the head.

1 Begin with Basic Shape VII (p.54), open point downwards.

3 ... fold the bottom point up. Repeat on the reverse side.

6 Roll the wings around a pencil to give them shape.

2 Fold the front lefthand triangle over to meet the right one. Repeat on the reverse side. Along the dotted line...

4 Pull the right and lefthand points out to the sides. Fold to hold them in place. Make a crease along the horizontal white line.

7 Hold the crane's breast and gently move its tail to make it flap its wings.

STARS

STAR A

6 … open it out and press it apart. Fold it flat.

1 Begin with Basic Shape VII (p.54), open point upwards.

2 Fold the lower front point up to the top. Turn the shape over.

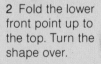

3 Along the dotted lines, fold the top two points …

4 … down to the sides and back up again.

7 Repeat with the righthand wing.

5 Lift the lefthand wing to the vertical …

8 Stick three stars on top of one another to make star A.

STAR B

3 Fold the lefthand point up through the centre on the top. Close the lefthand side.

6 Pick up the shape, holding the back and front wings together at the corners.

1 Start the Basic Shape VII (p.54), open point downwards.

4 Repeat with the righthand side. Along the dotted lines …

7 Pull the wings gently apart …

2 Open out both wings on the lefthand side.

5 … fold the lower front edges up to the centre line. Repeat on the back.

8 … until a square appears in the middle.

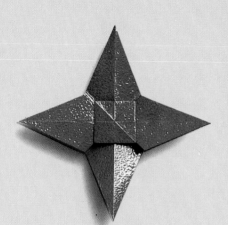

9 Press the shape flat and turn it over.

12 Open it out and press it apart.

15 Open the folds. Pull the point up gently.

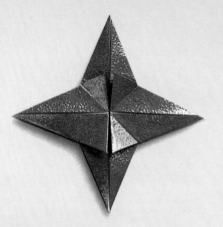

10 Take one of the four small central triangles ...

13 Repeat with the other three triangles. Along the dotted lines ...

16 Push the corners in to the centre. Repeat all round the star. Turn it over.

11 ... and lift it vertically.

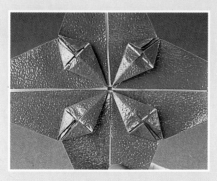

14 ... fold the short edges in to meet at the centre. Make a crease along the dotted lines.

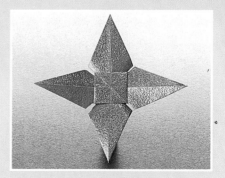

17 This is star B.

RABBIT

5 Along the dotted line …

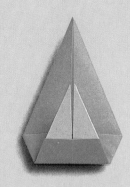

6 … fold the shape up.

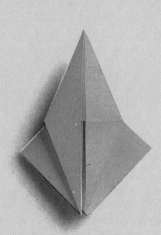

1 Begin with step 7 of Basic Shape VII (p.54). Turn the shape over.

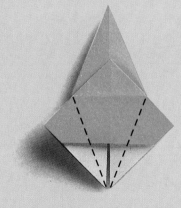

3 … fold the lower front triangle to the inside. Along the dotted lines …

7 Fold the shape in half so that both points are on the outside. Turn the shape so that they point to the right. Lift both points gently upwards …

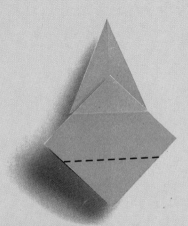

2 Along the dotted line …

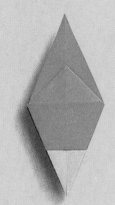

4 … fold the lower left and righthand sections inwards. Turn the shape over.

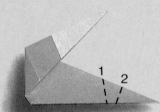

8 … and press the shape flat. Make sharp creases on the dotted lines.

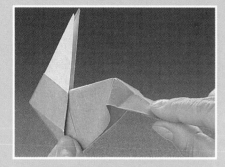

9 Fold the point inwards on the first crease . . .

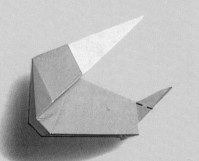

10 . . . and outwards on the second crease.

11 Make a crease on the dotted line.

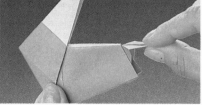

12 Fold the tail down through the crease you have just made.

13 Fold each ear downwards on the dotted line.

14 Make a crease on the dotted line. Repeat on the other side.

15 Turn in the corners on the creases you have just made.

16 Open out the ears . . .

17 . . . and fold them forwards.

18 Make a sharp crease on each ear on the dotted line.

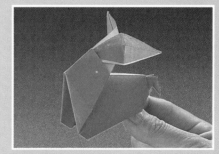

19 Open out the ears again, and the rabbit is ready.

2 ... and open them out until ...

3 ... the paper is quite flat.

DEVIL MASK

1 Begin with Basic Shape VII (p.54), the open point to the left. Take both the lefthand points ...

4 Turn it over. Along the dotted lines ...

5 ... press both upright points together in the middle and ...

6 ... run your thumbnails down the creases to the base.

7 Fold the paper in the middle.

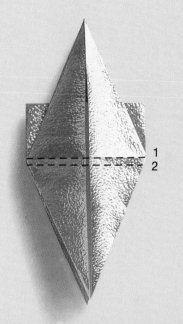

1
2

8 Make two parallel creases along the dotted lines. Fold the lower front triangle up to the inside on crease 1 and ...

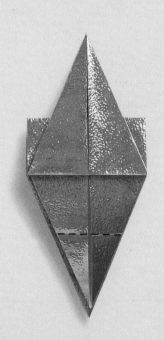

9 ... down to the outside on crease 2. Along the dotted line, fold the lower front triangle up.

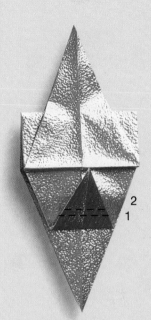

2
1

10 Make two parallel folds along the dotted lines.

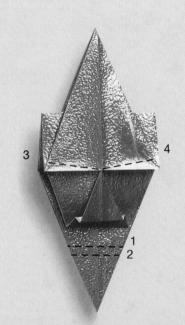

3　　4

1
2

11 Fold the triangle down on line 1 and up on line 2 to make the nose. Fold the lower triangle up on line 1 and down on line 2 to make the mouth. For the eyebrows fold the paper up along dotted lines 3 and 4. Fold the corners of the eyebrows down along these dotted lines.

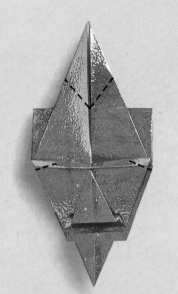

12 For the horns, fold the two points downwards along the dotted lines . . .

14 Fold the horns back up again, open them out . . .

17 Open the beard out a bit . . .

15 . . .and turn them in on the crease you have just made.

13 . . . to the right and left.

16 Repeat steps 13–15 on the points of the horns at the dotted lines. Turn the mask over.

18 . . . and press it flat.

19 Fold the mask in half. Along the dotted line ...

21 Turn the upper part of the face to the inside along the crease you have just made. Open it out.

23 ... fold the horns forwards. Release them.

20 ... make a crease.

22 Along the dotted lines ...

24 Shape the nose, and the mask is finished.

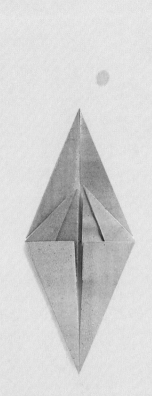

3 ... fold the lower edges in to the centre fold.

FOX MASK

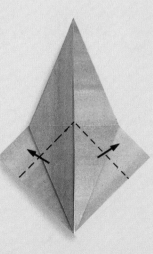

1 Begin with step 7 of Basic Shape VII (p.54). Along the dotted lines ...

2 ... fold the two lower front wings up to the horizontal. Along the dotted lines ...

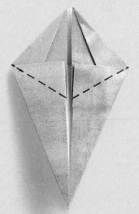

4 Fold the top point back on the horizontal centre fold. Along the dotted lines ...

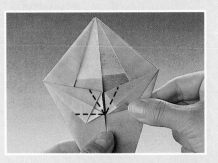

8 Fold the corners of the resulting shapes in on the dotted lines to the centre.

11 ... and press the corners in to the centre. Press them flat.

5 ... fold the two centre corners down.

6 Fold them back up again, stand them vertical ...

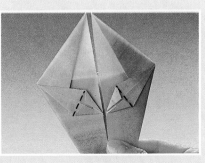

9 Make thumbnail creases along the dotted lines.

12 Along the dotted line ...

7 ... open them out and press them flat.

10 Open out the folds ...

13 ... fold the lower front point up. Along the dotted lines ...

14 … fold both points over to the left.

15 Unfold them again. Fold the front point up as in step 13 and fold both points over to the right …

16 … on the crease lines you have just made.

17 Open out the folds again, and fold the point up as before.

18 Lift the points up, press them together in the middle and …

19 … make firm creases down to the base.

20 Fold the shape in half with the points protruding.

21 Open out the ears and press down at the back to keep them open.

22 The fox mask is finished.

DESERT SCENE

CAMEL

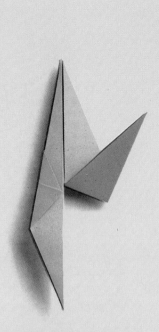

3 ... fold the lower righthand triangle up. Unfold it.

4 Separate the righthand wings ...

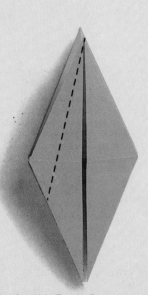

1 Begin with Basic Shape VII (p.54), open point downwards. Along the dotted line ...

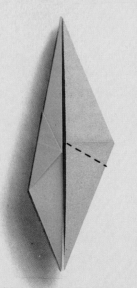

2 ... fold the front left wing forwards and the back left wing backwards to the centre. Along the dotted line ...

5 ... and push the point up on the crease you have just made.

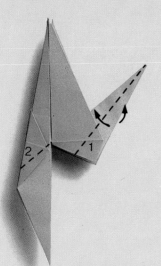

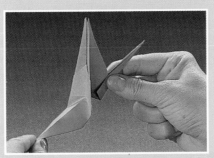

8 ... and fold the point up on the crease you have just made.

11 Open the folds of the righthand point again. Fold the middle wing along the dotted line ...

6 On dotted line 1, fold the front outer section back to the left. Make a sharp crease on dotted line 2.

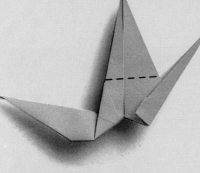

9 Along the dotted line ...

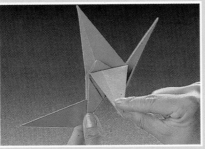

12 ... to the right and press down the resulting triangle.

7 Open the lefthand wing ...

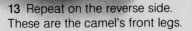

10 ... fold the top points to the front and back.

13 Repeat on the reverse side. These are the camel's front legs.

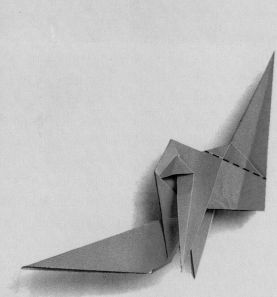

14 Make a sharp fold along the dotted line.

17 … backwards at dotted line 1. At dotted line 2, fold the lefthand wing up …

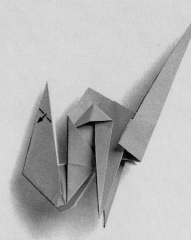

20 Fold the top left point over, making a sharp crease on the dotted line. Fold it back.

15 Lift up the front leg and push the corner in behind it. Repeat on the reverse side.

18 … unfold it and open out the point.

21 Open out the point and fold the top over …

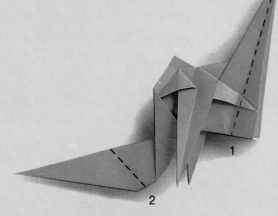

16 Fold the front of the righthand wing forwards and the back …

19 Fold the point back over the crease you have just made.

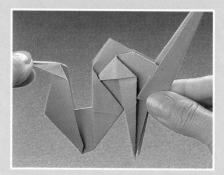

22 … to the left on the crease you have just made.

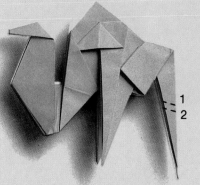

23 Press the neck in towards the body a little. Fold the righthand point over on the dotted line.

26 Make two parallel creases on the dotted lines.

29 The camel is finished.

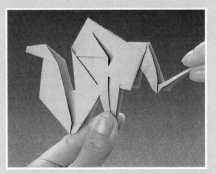

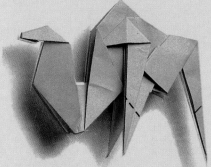

24 Fold it back and open out the wing.

27 Open out the wing. Push the point up through the first crease ...

30 If you want to make the camel sit down, fold the forelegs to the right and the back legs to the left.

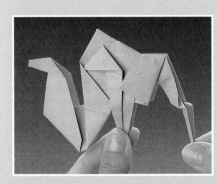

25 Fold it down inwards through the same crease.

28 ... and fold it down through the second to make the back legs.

31 The sitting camel looks like this.

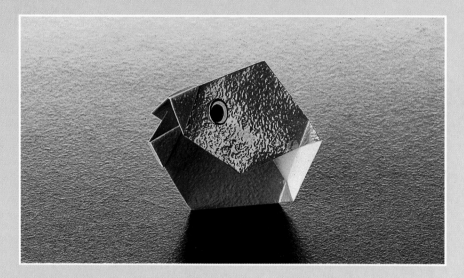

7 Hold the shape at either end and carefully put the right end-folds over the left end-folds.

TALKING FISH

1 Take a rectangular sheet of paper. The width must be less than half the length. Fold it along the dotted line.

4 Turn the shape over. Fold the points on the dotted lines ...

8 Hold the mouth of the fish and push the centre crease in from the back.

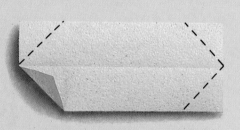

2 Lay the paper coloured side down. Fold all four corners in on the dotted lines ...

5 ... in towards the centre.

9 Align the two lower edges of the shape and press it flat.

3 ... to the centre.

6 Fold the shape in half with the white side of the paper inside.

10 Paint or stick on the eyes. Fold the tail over a little bit at both sides. The fish will speak when you pull gently on both sides of its tail.

MONKEY

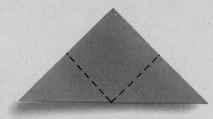

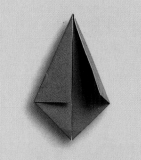

1 Make a triangular sheet of paper by cutting a square sheet diagonally in half. Make creases on the dotted lines.

3 ... fold the outer triangles in to meet at the centre. Unfold.

5 ... and fold the outer part of the left half in on the crease you have already made.

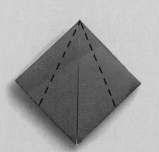

2 Fold the lower triangles up to meet at the centre. Along the dotted lines ...

4 Open the left half of the shape ...

6 Fold the left half of the paper together again.

7 Repeat steps 4–6 with the right half of the shape.

10 … and fold the top point over to the right.

13 Fold the monkey's right arm up. Fold the head in on the first crease, out on the second and in again on the third.

8 Fold the shape in half with the unfolded side of the paper inside. Turn it over. Along the dotted line, fold the front wing to the right …

11 Open the point and fold it down flat to the left. This is the head.

14 Open out the monkey's left arm from beneath.

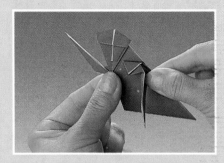

9 … and the back wing to the left. These are the arms. Fold the arms in half by folding the top part down at the centre. Turn the shape over …

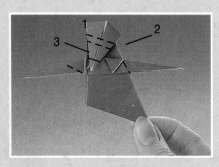

12 Make creases along the dotted lines.

15 Fold the lower part of the arm in on the crease you have already made.